The Healing Gift of Gratitude

*Live a happier, more peaceful life with
a unique practice of gratitude*

Shannon Elhart

BALBOA.
PRESS

A DIVISION OF HAY HOUSE

Balboa Press books may be ordered through booksellers or by contacting:

Balboa Press
A Division of Hay House
1663 Liberty Drive
Bloomington, IN 47403
www.balboapress.com
1 (877) 407-4847

Because of the dynamic nature of the Internet, any web addresses or
links contained in this book may have changed since publication and
may no longer be valid. The views expressed in this work are solely those
of the author and do not necessarily reflect the views of the publisher,
and the publisher hereby disclaims any responsibility for them.

The author of this book does not dispense medical advice or prescribe the use
of any technique as a form of treatment for physical, emotional, or medical
problems without the advice of a physician, either directly or indirectly. The
intent of the author is only to offer information of a general nature to help
you in your quest for emotional and spiritual well-being. In the event you use
any of the information in this book for yourself, which is your constitutional
right, the author and the publisher assume no responsibility for your actions.

Any people depicted in stock imagery provided by Thinkstock are
models, and such images are being used for illustrative purposes only.
Certain stock imagery © Thinkstock.

Print information available on the last page.

ISBN: 978-1-5043-6873-5 (sc)
ISBN: 978-1-5043-6874-2 (hc)
ISBN: 978-1-5043-6899-5 (e)

Library of Congress Control Number: 2016917994

Balboa Press rev. date: 12/16/2016

With Special Gratitude

Thank you to my parents, Ray and Vonnie Elhart, for loving and encouraging me through so many ups and downs. Your unending belief in me has helped me soar. I love you both dearly.

Thank you, Rayetta Perez and Stephanie Elhart, for your sisterhood and friendship. Without you both I wouldn't be where I am today, nor would this book. I love and appreciate you very much.

Missy Groothuis, you're an amazing friend who's cheered for me all along this journey. Thank you for listening and supporting my life and work. You are a gift in my life.

Sydra and Mack, you two hold the biggest parts of my heart. My gratitude for being your mom is so deep that I can hardly put it to words. I love you both more today than yesterday - and that will be true for each day that comes.

"Gratitude is the memory of the heart."

~ **Jean Baptiste Massieu**

Many authors explain that their books were labors of love. *The Healing Gift of Gratitude* is the result of my Labor of Desperation.

In one decade I experienced: my baby's death after a terminal pregnancy, facing my addiction to alcohol head on, divorce (and about every sour result from that), moving to a new home, single mom adjustments, painfully deep loneliness, healing from rape (twenty years after it occurred), a loved one's swift decline into dementia, unemployment and the desire to create my dream business (without any business education or experience), financial uncertainty (to put it lightly), and a search to end a lifelong struggle with a lack of self-worth.

I was often desperate to find inner peace, hope, and happiness. I wanted to heal the pain from my past so I could step more fully into my life.

There were occasions when I raised my fists in frustration and asked "*Why me? Why so much pain and struggle?*"

But even when those questions popped up during moments of self pity or anger, there was a significantly louder voice saying, "*Look deeper. Look within. Things will get better.*"

Sometimes the voice would elaborate, "*Shannon, when you can pull your perspective out of fear, you'll see a bigger picture. You can find a purpose, even a gift. Allow your life to unfold without trying to control everything."* Sometimes it was very brief, *"Trust."*

I listened to that voice even when I didn't want to. In hindsight, I see that my labor of desperation was, indeed, a Labor of Love, and I'm grateful for every bit of it. I now love myself and my life - even the parts that have brought me to my knees.

My inspiration for writing this year-long journey is to create more gratitude in your life and to encourage you to heal any pain from your past. Within these pages I've created 48 ways you can find new perspectives and gratitude for your life, the people around you, and the entire world.

Each way to finding gratitude falls into one of three themes: Acknowledging Self, Appreciating Others, or Experiencing the World. My belief is that as you grow in gratitude for yourself and your personal life experiences, you'll open up more easily toward others and then the world. I've also included four special weeks that will encourage you to view your joy differently, and learn how happiness, peace, and love are things you can give freely to anyone and everyone in our world.

My suggestion for how you use this book is that you read one week's content per week - preferably on the same day of the week throughout the year. Then spend the seven days recording gratitude on the journaling pages that follow. Each week will present a different focus within a theme.

If you'd like some helpful and free additional resources, there's a web address at the back of each theme. Each address will direct you to a site where you can access information about self-forgiveness and forgiving others, how to remain more grounded in your life, guided meditations, how to live a life with more compassion for yourself and others, an extra, fun practice of gratitude, and how to heal the pain from your past. These are my gifts to you as I appreciate you reading my book!

With Love,

Shannon Elhart

Acknowledging Self

"That man is rich whose pleasures are the cheapest."

~ **Henry David Thoreau**

Money. It seems to be one of the largest stressors in our world. Most people never feel they have enough, and the anxiety grows. Yet, when asked what they cherish most, it's rarely something of monetary value. When someone is on their death bed, their wishes rarely focus on missing out on *things*. Rather they yearn to have had more time with loved ones, to have relaxed and enjoyed each day more, to have been more passionate about life. As life comes to an end, we yearn to have experienced much joy. Create that now in your life, so you look back with a smile rather than regret.

We're all surrounded with natural opportunities to feel joy. Just step outside to walk in the forest or hear the chirping of birds, and you'll find a calming in your heart.

Even within your home you can find simple pleasures. You might relax in a hot shower or bubble bath or lose yourself in a great novel. Work in a garden, cook a great meal, play a board game with loved ones, sip on a cup of tea, or spend some time on a hobby... these are all easy, free ways to enjoy yourself.

This week be grateful for the many options you have to enjoy life. Each day list something you can do that costs nothing but time. You choose how to spend each moment: remain at a frenzied pace, or be empowered by slowing down and finding pleasure in simple, free joys.

Like most people, you might get wrapped up in technology. Although technology creates convenience, fun and connection, it's also very draining - especially on time. For this week of expressed gratitude, list no more than one free joy that involves technology. Choose some free joys that involve friends, nature, or simple ways to relax alone.

Week starting:

Day 1

Day 2

Day 3

Day 4

Day 5

Day 6

Day 7

Reflections on my week of gratitude

"Keep all special thoughts and memories for lifetimes to come. Share these keepsakes with others to inspire hope and build from the past, which can bridge to the future."

~ **Mattie Stepanek**

It's so much fun to recall special memories! Everyone's had experiences that make them smile. These experiences could be simple - a meaningful conversation with a loved one, or more extravagant - a vacation to an exotic destination.

Each memory is unique. Even events shared with others are captured in a personal way. Emotions, perspectives, and moments of time are yours alone. You can revisit memories stored in your mental photo album any time you choose.

Peacefully page through an album of mental memories and feel yourself soften in body and mind. When special moments are recalled, drift away from today's events and immerse yourself in the memory all over again. Your life has so many 'good times' to celebrate!

This week, remember seven very special times in your life, and express why you're grateful for each... remind yourself of how your life is blessed in countless ways.

This week keep your mind on positive memories. If you drift to a memory that creates sadness, turn to another. If you find yourself wishing to relive a time or to bring back someone who has passed away, turn your emotions to the pleasure and gift of this experience or person in your life. For at least one day this week, think of a special memory you'd like to create in the future... then plan for it!

Week starting:

Day 1

Day 2

Day 3

Day 4

Day 5

Day 6

Day 7

Reflections on my week of gratitude

"Believe in yourself! Have faith in your abilities! Without a humble but reasonable confidence in your own powers you cannot be successful or happy."

~ **Norman Vincent Peale**

Every person has abilities and talents. Do you ever consider what helps you feel confident? That's not vanity, it's healthy!

What are you good at? What are you drawn to because it's fun or easy or beneficial to the world? What comes naturally to you? What have you devoted time to learning so you could do it more or better?

It might be an innate talent or a learned skill. Perhaps you're a great cook or talented host. Maybe you're skilled in the arts or in sports. Have you developed a knack for writing poetry, gardening, or organizing? Do people or animals easily feel comfortable in your presence? Do you decorate your home with ease and flair? Do others come to you to get help with problems because you're always a good listener? Maybe you're great at developing solutions for issues at home or work.

The more we focus on our talents, skills, and passions - anything we find as an inherent talent or a learned skill - the better we feel about ourselves. Spend time thinking about your abilities and strengths. You might even ask people you trust to share what they believe are your strongest attributes.

Each day this week, write down one talent, skill, or ability and why or how you're grateful for it. What abilities allow you to shine in the world? How do you use each ability in your life or how could you use it more?

Have fun each day as you list some of your talents and abilities. For at least one day, recall one skill you've worked hard to master. Perhaps it did not start out as a natural ability, but over time and with effort, it has become a real source of talent.

Week starting:

Day 1

Day 2

Day 3

Day 4

Day 5

Day 6

Day 7

Reflections on my week of gratitude

"Gratitude is not only the greatest of virtues, but the parent of all others."

~ Marcus Tullius Cicero

Focusing on specific and personal reasons to find gratitude opens your mind to expressing appreciation for all of life and the world. As you express gratitude in each day's moments, you give birth to more peace and optimism.

This week reflect upon your daily events and be grateful for one thing. Each day brings blessings, even days you might think of as difficult or frustrating. When you find gratitude in each day of life, you're blessed with more peace, comfort, joy and trust in all you experience.

Your gratitude might be for something often overlooked, like the sun sparkling through the trees or for something you're typically not grateful for like the rain. It could even be for a difficult experience, such as an argument that provided you with an opportunity to use your voice in a loving way or to find tolerance or forgiveness. You might even realize that such a difficult experience gave you a chance to reflect on how to respond with more trust knowing every experience is an opportunity to learn.

As you feel gratitude, reflecting on all you experience, your day will end in a way that brings you empowerment and peace. This daily practice brings a more joyful day to day life.

As you spend time each day finding something to be grateful for, also record appreciation for one thing that upset you this week. Finding a gift in this experience - trusting there is a silver lining, a purpose, or a simple lesson - will move the dark clouds, allowing the sun to shine peacefully upon you.

Week starting:

Day 1

Day 2

Day 3

Day 4

Day 5

Day 6

Day 7

Reflections on my week of gratitude

"The advantage of the emotions is that they lead us astray."

~ Oscar Wilde

Each moment of every day, you are experiencing an emotion. When it feels like you're not, you're likely feeling calm and peaceful. If only life was filled with only those two emotions -- but it isn't.

There are many ways in which our emotions can become uncomfortable. The feelings of anger or jealousy, hopelessness or grief, anxiety or stress, can arise from all sorts of life experiences. Emotional triggers are different for everyone. What upsets you might not even be noticed by someone else, that's why it's important to accept all your emotions - and the emotions of others - without judgement.

However, even without judging an emotion, you may become carried away with it. When that happens, it's difficult to accept and learn from it. Each of your emotions is a guidepost to your life. Any feeling that arises will guide you to your next decision, action, or spoken word. When the emotion seems too powerful to allow you the comfort of making a conscious decision, it's important to first find calm.

Depending on the emotion that seems to carry you away - create a plan for calm. If you struggle with anger, decide what you can do when it arises. Lace up your running shoes and go for a jog or breathe and stretch with yoga. If deep sadness appears, hit the trail for a nature walk or let your tears flow as you write in a journal. If hopelessness is stealing the joy from your day, perhaps a soothing bubble bath or a vulnerable conversation with a trusted friend will lift the darkness. Fear, the foundation of all uncomfortable emotions, is quieted by silencing any negative chatter in your mind or by listing all the ways in which you have overcome challenging life experiences.

This week, your goal is to create a simple plan for handling these seven emotions: anger, sadness, anxiety, hopelessness, worry, jealousy, and fear. This will allow you to be *with* the emotion in a personally meaningful way that does not cause you to become *lost* in the emotion. Record in your journal your personal plan and why you're grateful to have this choice when coping with each uncomfortable emotion.

Although you may rarely feel an emotion listed during this week - make a plan for it anyway. All emotions are purposeful in guiding your life, so it's very likely that each emotion will arise at one time or another. Empower yourself to welcome and work with it, rather than let it carry you away.

Week starting:

Day 1

Day 2

Day 3

Day 4

Day 5

Day 6

Day 7

Reflections on my week of gratitude

"What you get by achieving your goals is not as important as what you become by achieving your goals."

~ **Henry David Thoreau**

You've probably heard, and likely commented yourself, "Time flies by so quickly!" It seems that with each passing year, the days slip away in a rush. It's easy to get caught up with the pace of day to day living and miss out on personal goal setting and dreaming. Unfortunately most people have said, "I've always wanted to..." or "I can't believe another year (or decade) has passed, and I've still not..."

This week spend time thinking about the goals, dreams or aspirations you hope to experience or accomplish in life. These might relate to your work or personal life - relationships, travel, or fun.

Maybe you'd like to learn how to scuba dive and go on an adventure in the tropics. Or perhaps you dream of writing a book. You might want to take a cooking class so you can throw one grand dinner party in your life. Dream away! What have you always longed to do, experience, learn, or try just once?

Your dreams might focus on out of the ordinary experiences or conjure up ideas that push your comfort zone, like acting in a play or bungee jumping. Perhaps it's someone you wish to meet. Maybe you want to learn how to play the violin, create watercolor paintings, or learn another language.

Life is wonderful, and although it might feel as though it passes too quickly, recognize how much choice you have in the creation of your life. Don't be someone who says, "I can't believe another year has passed, and I've still not..." Instead bring your dreams closer to reality by stepping forward, looking for opportunities, taking healthy risks, and authentically dreaming of what will put a big smile on your face.

Each day this week, add to your list of goals and dreams, and express gratitude for your ability to create life experiences. It's never too late to dream!

As you dream this week, and share gratitude for the ability to create life experiences, make one of your dreams big! Come up with at least one that might seem insurmountable but is exciting to imagine coming true!

Week starting:

Day 1

Day 2

Day 3

Day 4

Day 5

Day 6

Day 7

Reflections on my week of gratitude

"Circulating through the children's ward and seeing terminally ill kids, heads shaved, smiling and having a ball despite the tubes and needles sticking in them, I thought: 'What do I have to worry about? If God takes me, at least I've lived for 35 years."

~ **Eric Davis**

You're going to put a twist on your thinking this week. You have probably heard stories that broke your heart, urged you to hug your loved ones more tightly, or encouraged you to count your blessings. The news sometimes reminds us that there is unspeakable pain in the world. Every day there are people who are hungry, frightened, fighting through a serious illness, lacking shelter, or experiencing trauma.

When you learn about sad or frightening news in the world, it's powerful to realize all you have to be grateful for, and it's important to find gratitude for what you do *not* have or have *not* experienced.

Perhaps you've not experienced a horrible accident, financial uncertainty, or deep loneliness. Maybe you have not lost a dearly loved one or coped through a serious illness or injury. Many people have never experienced the lack of simple, daily needs such as clean water, healthy food, or safe shelter, but too many people - worldwide - deal with these issues each day.

Each day this week, think of something you've *not* had to struggle through. Express gratitude for these things you do *not* have or have *not* experienced as suffering or challenges.

As you feel gratitude for not having experienced something - things that people in the world deal with every day - go one step further. At one point this week, think of a way in which you can help others who are struggling. Perhaps you can donate some time or money, or maybe spend sincere time in prayer to lift those who do struggle.

Week starting:

Day 1

Day 2

Day 3

Day 4

Day 5

Day 6

Day 7

Reflections on my week of gratitude

"Gratitude makes sense of our past, brings peace for our today, and creates a vision for tomorrow."

~ **Melody Beattie**

This week marks the eighth week of your journey with The Healing Gift of Gratitude, and the second week for expressing gratitude about your day.to.day life.

Your goal this year is to create a habit of day to day, even moment to moment, gratitude. Living with the near constant expression of thankfulness for simple pleasures - the sunshine or a friendly hello from a passing stranger - creates a fulfilling and peaceful life.

The hope is that this gratitude and subtle shift in perspectives will also begin your journey to heal any pain from your past that still affects your present life.

Throughout this week, end each day lifting your spirits by recalling things to be grateful for. There might be days when this feels difficult, when nothing seems to go right, when you feel defeated, depressed, angry, or hopeless... Do it anyway! On a supposed bad day, find something to smile about, even if it's a glimpse of sunshine on a stormy afternoon. Each stormy day moves into your past as soon as you rest your eyes. In the morning you'll have the opportunity to experience a fresh day.

As you find gratitude each day this week, encourage others to share their own sentiments of gratefulness. It's simple, all you need to do is ask, "What's been good about your day so far?"

Week starting:

Day 1

Day 2

Day 3

Day 4

Day 5

Day 6

Day 7

Reflections on my week of gratitude

27

"If everyone would look for that uniqueness then we would have a very colorful world."

~ **Michael Schenker**

When you hold a candle to no one but yourself, it's easier to see how you shine brightly. You might be tempted to compare yourself to others, but in doing so, you cast a shadow on your authentic uniqueness.

There's no reason to compare yourself to anyone. As Deepak Chopra says, *"There are no extra pieces in the universe. Everyone is here because he or she has a place to fill, and every piece must fit itself into the big jigsaw puzzle."*

You are a piece of that puzzle. Your life has purpose, even if that purpose is not recognized by many. Without you, the world is missing an important piece.

When you focus on what makes you unique, authentic... what makes you YOU... what do you see? Do you see physical attributes like a fabulous smile, wild curly hair, bright sparkly eyes, or strong arms ready to help others or give a loving hug? Or are there ways in which your talents and strengths make you stand out from those around you? Perhaps you're very good at keeping things organized or at throwing a wonderful birthday party for someone special. Maybe it's the fact that you know a lot about the world's history, that you're always willing to lend a helping hand, or that you can make anyone feel at home in a new crowd of people.

What makes you stand tall, confident, and assured that you're great just the way you are? If you can change something that steals your confidence, change it. If you wish you were in better physical shape, then create a plan to eat healthier and workout. But if you dislike your nose or how tall you are, stop giving it any attention. Focus on what makes you feel good about who you are - a one of a kind person who's an important piece of the puzzle in our world.

Every day this week, express gratitude for one of the personal qualities that makes you unique and authentic. Remind yourself to focus on each of these qualities to increase your confidence and your ability to help create a better world.

This week, as you reflect on your reasons to feel confident, think about what others say about you (if you need to, ask some trusted friends). What do people compliment you on the most? Write it down and feel good that it's a natural part of you!

Week starting:

Day 1

Day 2

Day 3

Day 4

Day 5

Day 6

Day 7

Reflections on my week of gratitude

"When you've seen beyond yourself, then you may find, peace of mind is waiting there."

~ **George Harrison**

Everyone struggles. Every person has days that are difficult, frustrating, or depressing. That's part of life - the nonduality of your experience. In order to appreciate the good stuff you must also experience the bad stuff.

It can be easy to get caught up in the bad stuff or the struggles, especially when they seem constant or powerful. Of course there are days when it might feel like you have no choice - when you feel there is no option but to struggle or feel upset. Yet, don't allow these times to define you or your life. There's a choice every day as to which emotion - peace or frustration - you'll carry through those 24 hours.

What is peace? It's that ability to remain calm, in mind, emotion and action, regardless of what's happening around you. It's not always easy to do; it takes practice, but it is a choice. Typically your mind runs with stories, often unwarranted, that bring you to an unpeaceful place. However, you can choose peace, and practice doing so whenever the opportunity arises. Having a plan helps you practice.

This week find gratitude for the many ways in which you can choose to be in peace. How you find peace is a personal part of your journey and a very valuable one to understand. You might find peace in listening to classical music or heavy metal. You might feel it as you walk on the beach, sit in the sunshine, or gaze at the night's moon. You might experience peace while speaking vulnerably with a reliable friend. Perhaps peace appears as you let a hot shower soak into your body or as you curl up with a book and a cup of hot tea beneath a cozy blanket. Maybe it's peaceful for you to bake your favorite cookie recipe passed down from your grandmother.

The key is to have a plan for those times in life when peace seems fleeting or impossible. When you need that plan, be sure to implement it!

This week, for at least one of the days, choose a peace action that you can do *anytime* and from *anywhere*. For example, your action might be to breathe with more awareness, pray, meditate, recall a favorite memory or envision yourself resting in the place you find most beautiful and calming. Maybe it's that treasured friend whom you call or the journal you pour your heart into. Be grateful for your personal path to peace.

Week starting:

Day 1

Day 2

Day 3

Day 4

Day 5

Day 6

Day 7

Reflections on my week of gratitude

"Develop an attitude of gratitude, and give thanks for everything that happens to you, knowing that every step forward is a step toward achieving something bigger and better than your current situation."

~ **Brian Tracy**

Giving thanks for everything that happens to you might feel like an impossibility. Yet, there is purpose, even in pain -- if not a purpose, there's always something to learn about yourself or about life. When life seems to overwhelm you with grief, fear, anger, hopelessness, or sadness, know it will pass. Realize that in these times, you're meant to learn and grow.

Kahlil Gibran, a philosopher and gentle spirit, spoke to this nonduality in life. Long ago he stated: *"The deeper that sorrow carves into your being, the more joy you can contain."*

This week open yourself to the depth sorrow has carved into your being. Begin to view this open space, made from life's circumstances, in a fresh way. Joy will fill this space, especially when you can see a possible purpose in your struggles.

Each day reflect on one struggle you've faced in life. Look at each event, whether it was for you to endure alone or with others, and search for a small bit peace within the experience. Find something to be grateful for regarding this pain - a gift, a purpose, personal growth or something you learned from enduring this time in your life.

Perhaps you grew as an individual - having become more forgiving, trusting, honest, authentic, or accepting. Maybe you realized how strong you are, how blessed or cared for. During some difficult time, there was, perhaps, an opportunity for you to experience kindness from others. There may be ways you grew from pain into a more confident person, knowing what you stand for, your morals and values, your purpose and passion for life.

Struggles in life are unavoidable, and they're purposeful. There are no reasons for you to hold onto the past, especially if you grasp onto anger, regret, shame, or unforgiveness. Choose to remain in this present moment. Finding gratitude, even for your struggles, helps free you to enjoy today and the future.

*If you don't have seven struggles to reflect upon this week, consider the struggles of someone whom you care about, and find ways in which perhaps there was purpose in their life event. You don't need to share your ideas with these people, you need only send them love, peace, and hope from your heart.

This entire week might feel challenging but be courageous and trusting. You'll begin a journey of healing, and it's worth it. If you want to bring your healing a bit further, sit with a trusted friend and share the experience you're reflecting upon and how you're searching for inner peace.

Week starting:

Day 1

Day 2

Day 3

Day 4

Day 5

Day 6

Day 7

Reflections on my week of gratitude

"As we express our gratitude, we must never forget that the highest appreciation is not to utter words, but to live by them."

~ **John F. Kennedy**

Sunshine, rain. Kind words leading to a smile, harsh words encouraging patience. Ease, struggle. Success, failure. Dreams realized, endings accepted. Love, Fear. Friendship, discord.

Life is full of nondualities, and it must be. With these, you learn, grow, and appreciate the good parts of life more sincerely and passionately. It's possible to find deeper compassion for those who suffer while you're flourishing. In experiencing the tough stuff, you're able to touch your strongest, most optimistic self. You're empowered by finding gratitude in all of life's experiences.

For your twelfth week of The Healing Gift of Gratitude, express appreciation for each of your days. At the end of every day, find one reason for thankfulness and record it; your spirit and soul will be lifted, and rest will come more easily. If you experience a day which doesn't provide simple joy, know that you'll grow from it and awaken to a fresh start: darkness is overcome by light; the sun always rises.

Express gratitude, at least once this week, for someone whose behavior or choices frustrate or anger you. It might feel counterintuitive, but in doing so, you'll step toward acceptance and forgiveness -- two wonderful lessons in life.

Week starting:

Day 1

Day 2

Day 3

Day 4

Day 5

Day 6

Day 7

Reflections on my week of gratitude

"We can do no more without spirituality than we can do without food, shelter, or clothing."

~ **Ernest Holmes**

Many cultures generally focus on one or two parts of self: the physical body and the emotions. There is a vital part of self that greatly enhances the well-being of your physical form and emotional stability - your spirit.

One of the most meaningful areas of your life is your spirituality. You might define it through a religion, a connection with nature, a sense of community, or personal study. Regardless of how you view your spirit and spirituality, it's vital that you nurture and support it. As Holmes reflected, without such a connection, it's like trying to survive without adequate food or shelter.

How do you nourish your spirit? Do you read sacred texts such as the Bible, Qur'an, or Torah? Do you find enjoyment in reading spiritual poetry or scripture found in the Bhagavad Gita, the sutras, or the Tao Te Ching? Maybe it's the pure joy of connecting with others, walking in nature or reading the beautiful words of Thoreau.

Your spirituality and connection with the Divine are powerful comforts and guides in your life. In the hustle and bustle of many cultures, it's easy to overlook the importance of cultivating and replenishing that connection.

Perhaps you enjoy a walk in nature listening to the sounds of rustling leaves or chirping birds. Maybe you awaken each morning expressing gratitude to God or the universe before you lift your head from the pillow. For some it's a special routine of prayer and meditation, or attending a church, temple, or synagogue. Simple practices may foster your spirituality each day such as keeping a prayer list, taking time to breathe with awareness, moving through yoga postures, or slowing down to take in quiet moments and be mindful.

This week, find seven ways in which you currently connect to your spirit or will plan to begin doing so. Express gratitude for your freedom and ability to celebrate your spiritual essence in personally meaningful ways.

This is a very important part of each person's life - for wholeness and well-being. Even if you think you don't have time to cultivate your spirit, decide to add a few moments to each day in order to just 'be'. What simple act will you take to joyfully refresh your Spirit?

Week starting:

Day 1

Day 2

Day 3

Day 4

Day 5

Day 6

Day 7

Reflections on my week of gratitude

"The body is a sacred garment."

~ Martha Graham

You have one garment you'll wear your entire life. Given from Spirit, from God, from Life itself, your body is a true blessing and temple. Sure it will change with time: the form you might remember from earlier years is gone, perhaps with some changes you might not be fond of, but it's beautiful just the way it is today. Although you can't avoid changes - wrinkles around your eyes, slowing muscles, aching joints - there are many ways you *do* have choice.

What do you do to cherish and replenish your body? You likely have many options for food and exercise. That's not the case for the entire world's population. Many people are grateful simply for any source of food and their exercise is doing chores to maintain a basic level of comfort and necessity. Do you have choice? If so, what do you choose to do to honor your body?

Maybe you eat a very healthy diet or are diligent about vitamins and nutrients. You might be someone who enjoys regular exercise or a consistent schedule of rest. Perhaps you're good at using organic products or avoiding toxins. We all experience stress and anxiety at times; are you someone who has created healthy ways to cope by using relaxation, prayer, meditation, or time in nature?

If you find this challenging because you don't currently nurture your physical body, then come up with seven simple changes you can make over the next year and a plan to how you'll get started with each.

This week be grateful for the many ways you may choose to treat your body and cater to its strength and health. Each day list a way to honor your physical body by fostering its well-being.

As you think about ways in which you honor and strengthen your physical body, are there any ways in which you cause it harm? Are there habits to change or release? Would it benefit you to exercise more or learn healthy ways to cope with stress? If there is something you do that harms your body, take at least one day this week to record how you'll choose differently. You can be grateful not only for all you do to nourish your body, but also for your ability to choose the best ways to care for your sacred garment.

Week starting:

Day 1

Day 2

Day 3

Day 4

Day 5

Day 6

Day 7

Reflections on my week of gratitude

"I find hope in the darkest of days, and focus in the brightest. I do not judge the universe."

~ Dalai Lama

It's easy to find reasons to worry or feel hopeless about our world. As you listen to the news or tune in to conversations, you can easily hear pessimism. This might be expressed through anger or doubt, fear or depression. Tapping into that pessimism deflates your own joy and hope, and that of the world.

You might not think it matters if you're one more person in the world who feels a lack of hope. But you *do* matter, and so does your perspective. All of life is connected, and in that universal energy your state of hope has impact. Imagine if a single drop in an ocean represents each person needed to create the whole. Remove your drop and you might not see a difference, but if everyone removes their drop, that ocean would disappear.

All those drops, all those people - the majority can be of hope or of fear, of optimism or of hopelessness. Which will you choose?

You can choose to be someone who spreads the collective energy of joy, peace, love, and hope. You'll make a difference, and it will be noticed in how you speak to others, how you smile at strangers or lend a hand to someone in need, how you accept people rather than judge them, how your happiness - found in each moment of life - will spread to those you encounter. Your small drop of hope will be part of the whole.

What brings you hope?

Look at your immediate surroundings and the world at large. What is happening that brings a smile to your face? Who is a light to your life? Many inspiring people and organizations create positive change in the world... which ones give you hope?

If this is difficult for you, if you struggle to think of 'good' in the world - then turn off the television and any other source of news for this one week. You'll be fine; if any major world event occurs you'll learn of it. Even if it's easy for you to feel hope, try unplugging for one week. See how you feel before and after, and it's likely you'll feel more at peace after avoiding the negativity that's so easily mentally consumed by most people. You *do* have a choice of what information you allow into your mind, and that input affects how you feel each day. Choose peace. Choose optimism. Choose HOPE.

Week starting:

Day 1

Day 2

Day 3

Day 4

Day 5

Day 6

Day 7

Reflections on my week of gratitude

"At times our own light goes out and is rekindled by a spark from another person. Each of us has cause to think with deep gratitude of those who have lighted the flame within us."

~ **Albert Schweitzer**

Life is wonderful! You're blessed each day when you live fully - and it's your choice to do so. You may choose to find reasons to grumble or choose to find appreciation and happiness. It might not always be easy; there are days when life throws struggles your way. These times might last moments, days, weeks or months. But you always endure. You've gotten through each day of life so far, and most have been filled with opportunities for peace and joy.

You're learning and experiencing that now.... the ability to choose how you view life. When you shift to a perspective of gratitude, that perspective is reflected in how you treat others. As you create a better energy of love around yourself, you impact those around you with that love.

It's a circle - the infinite connection of all of life. What you give is returned to you. Choose gratitude, peace, love, and joy. Live an optimistic life!

When a day comes where optimism is hard to grasp, know there are others who care and will help light your flame again. The spark of hope is always available; appreciate receiving it as much as giving it to others.

This week express gratitude for your day to day life. Don't record only one thing to appreciate, instead, express two each day. In doing so, your body, mind and spirit will soften into the choice of optimism.

This week remember at least one person who lifts your spirit when you're having a down day - a person who seems to spark the light within others because she keeps her own light bright. Be thankful for those special people in your life.

Week starting:

Day 1

Day 2

Day 3

Day 4

Day 5

Day 6

Day 7

Reflections on my week of gratitude

"Out of suffering have emerged the strongest souls; the most massive characters are seared with scars."

~ **Kahlil Gibran**

We all have difficult times in life, and the cards are not stacked evenly. If you're someone who has experienced more struggles than most, it can feel very discouraging or even worrisome. If you're someone who's had a great hardship, it can feel like a darkness that might never fade.

To even think of finding a 'silver lining' or gift may be painful or frustrating. To think that there's purpose or a lesson in every life struggle might not feel like a possibility.

However, in life you always have choice. You can choose to hold on to painful events in the past with anger, pity, sadness, jealousy, self-doubt, or emptiness. You can choose to hold that pain for the rest of your life.

You can also choose to let it go, even bit by bit - like opening a handful of sand allowing some to fall, then re-gripping it tightly for a while longer before you again open your hand to release more. This opening and closing can continue, until eventually, you have an open and empty hand, free to grasp something new.

Acknowledging and witnessing your pain, finding anything 'good' or purposeful about your experience, determining a way in which you grew or learned from every life event - these are steps that allow your heart to open and clear the way for new love, joy, hope, and peace. Your choice soothes the scars and leaves you strengthened.

For this week, think about your toughest life experience. In reflecting about it, each day determine one way in which you grew, one thing you learned, one life lesson you had while traveling this valley of your life. It might be as simple, yet profound as, 'I learned to forgive' or 'I never felt others support me as much as I did during this time.'

Here's an example from my life: In the summer of 2000 I experienced a terminal pregnancy. My son, Jonathan, was born on September 21, and he died the following day. Through this challenging time, I experienced tremendous compassion; I realized that I am a very strong woman; I learned to trust God more deeply; I had the experience of letting go even when I did not want to which has helped me trust the unfolding of life; I learned how to create peace; I began embracing my authenticity; and I was blessed with time to cradle Jonathan in my arms and look in his beautiful eyes.

If strong pain arises, be sure to take time to be gentle with yourself - take a warm bath, go for a calming walk in nature, treat yourself to a massage. As you open your heart to the pain, go slowly and know that it can be replaced with peace.

Week starting:

Day 1

Day 2

Day 3

Day 4

Day 5

Day 6

Day 7

Reflections on my week of gratitude

"Opportunities multiply as they are seized."

~ Sun Tzu

The word 'opportunity' rings with possibility, excitement, adventure, or advancement. When you reflect on opportunities in your life, you might look for big events or changes - perhaps a trip abroad, a scholarship to further your education, or the chance encounter with a famed mentor you've admired from afar.

Opportunities in your life arrive all the time and in a variety of ways. To advance in your career, for example, can be exciting and fruitful. However, the simple, repeated occasion to quietly enjoy a sunset from a nearby beach is also a wonderful opportunity.

This week, look for opportunities you've seized and think about how they've multiplied in your life. Perhaps you've had countless chances to enjoy a particular event, like a sunset, making it an abundant pleasure. Or maybe a certain situation rippled through your life, leading to another and yet another experience that moved you forward or blessed you in some way.

You might even view opportunity as a synchronistic way your life has been guided. These can be subtle: the mention of a book during a casual conversation, that same book showing up on your coffee table after someone gave it to your spouse, and then that book leading you to exciting change in your personal life. These synchronicities can even be surprisingly packed with big change in your life: dreaming of a location, traveling to that exact spot later that year, then falling in love while there.

This week, take a fun walk through the pages of your life and look for the opportunities that have led you to today. Consider the more common ones - those you might easily overlook, but other people might be thrilled to experience. Take a moment each night to express gratitude for the countless opportunities that have blessed your life!

See if you can recall something that seemed like a terrible situation in your life at the time, but turned out to be a gift. Perhaps you lost your job and financially security, but you ended up learning a lot about what's really important to you, and you found a career you're much more passionate about.

Week starting:

Day 1

Day 2

Day 3

Day 4

Day 5

Day 6

Day 7

Reflections on my week of gratitude

"A day without laughter is a day wasted."

~ **Charlie Chaplin**

"A smile is a curve that sets everything straight."

~ **Phyllis Diller**

Leave it to two well-known comedians to identify two wonderful truths. Laughter and smiling... simple ways to lift any situation. Do you ever have a day when you don't laugh? A day when a smile never shows up on your beautiful face?

It *is* a day wasted when we don't find something to enjoy. There are days when we have to do just that: *find* a reason. There are days that are extraordinarily difficult - when a natural laugh or even a slight curve of a smile on your lips might feel impossible. Those are the days to search for that simple joy.

What or who in your life always brings a smile to your face? Is it a particular photograph of a loved one? Or maybe a quick phone call with a child or dear friend? It might be that a quick walk through the forest always makes you smile. Perhaps it's an adored pet who always makes you laugh. Maybe it only takes a particular television show or a simple treat like extra whipped cream on your latte to lift your spirits.

When you need to have a slight shift in your energy or outlook, when you crave a little lift to your mood - who or what can you turn to? This week consider people, things, or experiences that you can be grateful for because they bring you a hearty laugh or they put a smile on your face no matter what's happening in your life.

Be sure to recognize something you can do at *any* time and in *any* place that will bring you simple joy. It might be an image in your mind, a prayer or poem you recite quietly to yourself. Capturing a dependable source of joy to have at your beck and call is a gift!

Week starting:

Day 1

Day 2

Day 3

Day 4

Day 5

Day 6

Day 7

Reflections on my week of gratitude

"The desire of gold is not for gold. It is for the means of freedom and benefit."

~ **Ralph Waldo Emerson**

I think it would be quite difficult, near impossible, to live without desire. We desire all the time - a cup of coffee to start our morning, a conversation to go a certain way, a work day to end with all tasks complete, time to enjoy a new book, a fun vacation, a great love relationship, or even a new pair of fabulous shoes.

We desire things, relationships, and experiences.

But what we *really* desire are *feelings*.

We want to feel a certain way, and we believe that these things, experiences or people will cause us to capture that emotion. Funny thing is, once we grasp what we desire and maybe even bask in that emotion *for a while*... we find a new something or someone to desire, so we can feel that way again. We tend to chase *things* rather than *feelings*.

Each day we decide how we'll feel. Of course, when tragedy arises or a significant blow impacts our life, it's much more difficult to believe we have any choice. At those times, we must allow the emotions to arise without judgement and let that carry us to acceptance and eventually peace.

Danielle LaPorte teaches this concept of feeling what you want in her Desire Map. She states, "You can't always choose what happens to you, but you can always choose how you feel about it." At most times, thank goodness, you can choose *what happens* in your day to day life... You're empowered by

70

choice - and choosing will more likely result in your desired emotion.

Unfortunately, the pace of most societies feels too rushed; we experience life happening 'to us,' and we seem to 'just go through the motions' of each day. Put an end to that. Decide to be more purposeful in creating your life's experiences.

When we remember this power within ourselves - to choose - our desires begin to synchronize with our experiences. It's then that we have the power to feel happiness even if we don't have that one thing we believe will make us happy... to feel love even if we don't have that relationship we so deeply want... to feel confident even when life feels uncertain... and to feel peace simply because it's all around us. We learn to create circumstances that result in our desired emotion without relying on others, events, or accomplishments.

For each day this week, begin by thinking of something you desire - a new career, a passionate lover, a great friendship, to lose twenty pounds, more money, a cool sports car, a healed relationship, a day at a spa, a cute puppy... anything that sounds fulfilling, fun, or exciting to you.

After thinking about that one thing, decide how you would *feel* if it was to come into your life and record that in your journal. Then record at least two ways you could bring that feeling into your life more regularly. For instance, if you desire feeling at peace, these things might bring you peace: a quiet night reading a book, a walk on the beach, a soothing bath. If you desire fun with special people perhaps you could sign up for an art class, plan a casual bike ride with friends, or organize a monthly game night with family.

The late Debbie Ford encouraged people to plan something each month that would result in a special memory. This can be a simple, free event - something alone or with people you care about. Take out your calendar - after the name of each month choose a special experience to create. It could be 'ride bikes with my kids to get ice cream' for the month of July or 'go the the opera' in February. Then make a commitment to yourself that you'll plan each event as the month arrives.

Extra (fun) Challenge: Take ten minutes to envision your life in 3-5 years. Who are you with? Where do you live? What are you doing? Get in touch with the feelings from what you envision. Hold that vantage point without the specific details of who, what, when, where, or how. Instead *hold the feeling*. Do this every day for a few moments - envision a glimpse of your future as your desire, then hold the emotion of that future, allow it to fill your body and soul.

Week starting:

Day 1

Day 2

Day 3

Day 4

Day 5

Day 6

Day 7

Reflections on my week of gratitude

"'Thank you' is the best prayer that anyone could say. I say it a lot. Thank you expresses extreme gratitude, humility, understanding."

~**Alice Walker**

For this Personal Daily Reflection we're going to do something a bit different. Most of us say 'thank you' quite often. But most of us also say these words without a lot thought about the power they yield.

'Thank you' is strong, but it also softens. It can put a smile on someone's face and encourage them to keep doing good in the world. It can express sincerity and kindness wrapped in gratitude. For two little words, together, they can create a lot of positive change.

This week you'll challenge yourself to use those words with a bit more awareness, purpose, and intention. You'll use these two words to feel good inside and to bring good to those around you.

Grab seven scraps of paper or sticky notes, and on each write 'Thank you.' Then post them in a variety of places: in your purse or wallet, on the rearview mirror of your car, on the window above your kitchen sink, on your desk or nightstand or laptop. These are your reminders to express thanks with a bit more intention this week.

Now each day, grab a note and keep it with you until you've expressed those two words - thank you - with a bit more gusto. Here are a few examples: to the person who bags your groceries look him in the eyes and say 'Thanks a lot for helping me - I really appreciate it' or to the taxi driver who brings you to a restaurant

'Thank you so much for driving me here and keeping me safe' or to your neighbor who's always so friendly, 'Thank you for being such a great neighbor. I appreciate your kindness and always enjoy our conversations' or even to your beloved, 'Thank you for loving me, for helping me succeed in life, and for creating a great life together.'

This week, write down the people who you express your sincere thanks to. Include how it felt for you to do so. You could even write down how the other person responded. Let those little words, 'thank you', carry a bit more power as you express them with a bit more sincerity and intention.

Our natural world could use a lot more gratitude spoken from the heart. Stop by nature while you're on a walk or just gazing out your window. You'll see a beautiful tree, the sunshine, a gorgeous flower, or a butterfly flutter past you - and say thank you from the depth of your heart.

Week starting:

_____

Day 1

_____

Day 2

_____

Day 3

_____

Day 4

Day 5

Day 6

Day 7

Reflections on my week of gratitude

Part of Acknowledging Self with gratitude means practicing self-forgiveness and learning how to have less anxiety in life.

I've created a free gift that'll teach you how to forgive yourself and reduce the anxiety you feel. I hope each blesses you abundantly!

Go to www.shannonelhart.com/gratitude-self to enjoy them!

Appreciating Others

"The fact that I can plant a seed and it becomes a flower, share a bit of knowledge and it becomes another's, smile at someone and receive a smile in return, are to me continual spiritual exercises."

~Leo Buscaglia

Inspiration - it's all around you, especially when you look closely. Take the time to slow down and be with the world - and you'll see how even a simple flower or a mighty tree inspires you to pause and enjoy a moment of peace.

As inconspicuously as nature inspires, people also inspire in simple ways that might go unnoticed. Who always finds the bright side to tough circumstances or difficult times? Who do you notice, even the grocery clerk at your local store, who wears a smile and shares a friendly hello? What person passes through your life always willing to help others without expectation?

There are bold achievements that might make us wonder how someone can affect others to such a great extent. You've likely heard about people who are doing great things - taking risks, using their voice, raising money for others in need, creating ways to help the world.

Who inspires *you*? What people, whether close or far away, inspire you to do more or act differently? Who makes you think of ways our world can become a better place?

This week think of one inspirational person each day. After writing his or her name, share what they're doing and a reason or two why you're grateful for their inspiration in the world.

80

As you list people who inspire you this week, be sure to think of at least one unexpected person who you interact with - even if only slightly. It might be the very helpful person at the doctor's office or the kind employee at the local market. Consider an unexpected person - someone who inspires others to be the best they can be in a very simple way - even through their genuine kindness.

Week starting:

Day 1

Day 2

Day 3

Day 4

Day 5

Day 6

Day 7

Reflections on my week of gratitude

"Let us be grateful for the people who make us happy; they are the charming gardeners who make our souls blossom."

~ **Marcel Proust**

You're blessed with people who you love easily; life is more complete and joyful because of them. You likely have family and friends who soften your heart when only thinking of them... just one thought - and you're smiling!

They bring you peace and hope. These wonderful people in your life bless you abundantly by simply being part of your journey. You probably can't imagine life without them.

Love is by far the most amazing gift in life.

This week spend time each day reflecting on these people. People might arise in your heart - parents, children, friends, even loved ones who have passed from this life. Think of specific reasons why you love and appreciate each person and record these on your journal pages.

Perhaps you love someone for their kindness or acceptance. Maybe you feel love toward someone for their tenderness, creativity, or for the way they always encourage you. Your love for someone could be an intuitive emotion, a connection between the two of you, or it might very simply and wonderfully just *be* love without any reasons or rationale.

As you reflect on all the people you love, and why, allow your heart to open to loving more deeply, more completely, and with more ease... knowing that this love you feel is a gift to your life and to theirs. Allow it to be given from you without expectation. As Marcel Proust states, these people are what make your soul blossom, and it's fun to express gratitude for their place in your life.

This week open your heart to experience love for someone whom it might be difficult to love. There is likely someone in your life who you feel has hurt you, and it might be difficult to feel love for this person. But be willing to open your heart, and find a reason to feel love for him or her.

Week starting:

Day 1

Day 2

Day 3

Day 4

Day 5

Day 6

Day 7

Reflections on my week of gratitude

"Feeling gratitude and not expressing it is like wrapping a present and not giving it."

~ **William Arthur Ward**

This is a special week with a little twist to your personal expressions of gratitude!

Last week, you wrote a reason or two for why you're grateful for the people who you love so easily and dearly.

Reflecting on why you're grateful for these wonderful people in your life was probably fun, and hopefully it put a smile on your face every day! It's a joy to think about why you love someone so deeply, and how you're grateful for this love in your life.

But there is something even better...

This week take your personal, written expressions of gratitude a bit further. Each day choose one of the people you wrote about last week and share with them - either verbally or in writing - the reasons why you're grateful to have them in your life. It could be a simple phone call, a quick note or email, or maybe a chance to share your feelings in person... including a big hug of gratitude!

In your journal this week, record how it felt to express gratitude to each person or how they responded to your gratitude. This is a wonderful and rewarding way to take those loving, grateful thoughts and give them away to those you love. The receiver of your kind expression will be uplifted... and so will you!

♥ **Gratitude Challenge:** Sharing Your Love

Is there someone overdue for your gratitude - perhaps someone who is in your life regularly but you often forget to share your appreciation. Maybe it's someone from long ago, whom you've always wished to thank but never found the time or words to do so. If someone you're grateful for has passed from this life or if it's uncomfortable for you to share, you can still express gratitude - just say a prayer or sit quietly while you feel love and gratitude in your heart and then pass it forward.

Week starting:

Day 1

Day 2

Day 3

Day 4

Day 5

Day 6

Day 7

Reflections on my week of gratitude

"Gratitude is the fairest blossom which springs from the soul."

~ **Henry Ward Beecher**

You're now living life from a deeper place of gratitude. As you see each day and every experience as a gift - even when you face difficulty - your life is constantly uplifted!

It's like finding a wilted flower and recognizing the beauty beneath its faded colors. When you do so, gratitude springs from your soul, even from such unexpected places.

This week find two reasons each day to express gratitude. As your day comes to an end, recall your waking moment and each event that followed. You might even recapture the smile that spread across your face as you drew back the curtains and watched sunshine stream in the room. Or perhaps it was the same first glance outside, but rather than sunshine your thankfulness was for the rain pouring from the sky. A sunny day, a rainy day... each a source of gratitude and an opportunity to be in love with life!

Little things, like receiving an unexpected compliment, sipping on a delicious milk shake, noticing a lovely butterfly flutter, or enjoying a common conversation, can create gratitude in your life. All around you there are reasons to find appreciation; share at least two from each day before you close your eyes to sleep.

If something happens this week that was unexpected, inconvenient, or unwanted, such as being very late for an appointment or work, express gratitude for accepting such detours in your day. Realizing that you're constantly guided gives you relief from your personal agenda. Perhaps forgetting your purse or wallet, then getting held up in traffic, was a way of saving you from a far worse predicament.

Week starting:

Day 1

Day 2

Day 3

Day 4

Day 5

Day 6

Day 7

Reflections on my week of gratitude

"An individual has not started living until he can rise above the narrow confines of his individualistic concerns to the broader concerns of all humanity."

~ **Martin Luther King, Jr.**

You make a difference in the world. Through kindness, forgiveness, compassion, and gratitude, you're able to make a bigger difference than you might realize.

There are people throughout the history of the world who've had a markedly positive effect on our global community. Every day there are people whose passion and purpose is to help others.

This week express gratitude for one person each day who has gifted our world. Your mind could run with people who have cured diseases, worked for more acceptance of human differences, sacrificed their own comforts to provide for others, created agencies and organizations that assist those in need. There's an abundance of people who have gifted our world.

Everyone is affected positively by the acts of these amazing people. Being thankful for the people you remember, and how they have provided so much to the world, is a way of keeping their goodness moving forward!

Although your mind is likely thinking about well-known people who've made a difference, remember - *you* can also have a positive impact. Whether one person or hundreds of thousands of people notice something you do to help the world does not matter. What can *you* do? This week think of something you'll do to bring more good to our world.

Week starting:

Day 1

Day 2

Day 3

Day 4

Day 5

Day 6

Day 7

Reflections on my week of gratitude

"I am a huge believer in giving back and helping out in the community and the world. Think globally, act locally. I believe the measure of a person's life is the affect they have on others."

~ **Steve Nash**

You might be surprised this week as you're encouraged to look for how you give to others. Serving others blesses you as much as it bless those you serve. This week look for all the ways you assist others.

Maybe you'll be reminded of simple, routine ways of service, such as making a healthy meal for your family, being kind to coworkers who are stressed, giving hugs to people you care about. Realize that your acts of kindness do not need to be enormous to carry a positive impact on the world.

There are ways people can serve with a greater impact. Opportunities to volunteer, assist an organization, or fund raise for an important cause are ways to assist your community or the world. Regardless of what you're able to do physically or monetarily, you can serve others in simple but meaningful ways - gifting others, but also giving to yourself.

This week be grateful for all the ways you give to others - you just might be surprised at what you find!

As you consider your own kind nature, also look at a new option for helping others. You could consider joining a small committee or a big venture which serves the world. Even tithing $10 a month can make a big impact. A simple and fun way to give to others is to say prayers or send loving energy to people who are struggling. That intentional, conscious act does make a difference in our world! Find one way in which you could serve others in the future.

Week starting:

Day 1

Day 2

Day 3

Day 4

Day 5

Day 6

Day 7

Reflections on my week of gratitude

"Without community service, we would not have the strong quality of life. It's important to the person who serves as well as the recipient. It's the way in which we ourselves grow and develop."

~ **Dorothy Height**

It's easy to find news that's depressing or frightening. Flip on the television or click on your computer, and you can discover news that brings you down. This week focus your gratitude on people and agencies that are doing good in your community.

There are many needs in our world and in every community - whether that be a small rural town or a bustling city with millions of people. There are people in your community who spend time creating programs to help children or the poor, who do what few others want to do, who volunteer or work for very little pay, simply to provide assistance to those in need. Everyone benefits from the tireless work of those who serve the community.

There are people in every country, city and community who strive to make their corner of the world a better place. In doing so, they're impacting our global community.

This week find inspiration from people who live near you, and use your journal to share gratitude for those people. Let's celebrate all the good their bringing the world!

This week search for an unexpected source of giving in your community. Perhaps you'll find an individual who goes out of his way to assist neighbors or a person who raises money in a simple way to purchase books for the nearby elementary school. Ask around - you might be inspired by the creativity of your neighbors' generous hearts.

Week starting:

Day 1

Day 2

Day 3

Day 4

Day 5

Day 6

Day 7

Reflections on my week of gratitude

"Gratitude unlocks the fullness of life. It turns what we have into enough, and more. It turns denial into acceptance, chaos to order, confusion to clarity. It can turn a meal into a feast, a house into a home, a stranger into a friend."

~ **Melody Beattie**

Like a treasure chest of simple joy, when you unlock each day by living in gratitude, every moment is better - more peaceful, more calm, more joyful. This is not necessarily taught in most homes or schools. Instead, it's more common to be inundated with the opposite: worry, overwhelm, stress, and desire.

Living with appreciation for all you have and experience releases that worry, overwhelm, stress, and desire. When you feel appreciation for each day, you don't feel the tension that often accompanies life.

You don't have to live waiting for something to happen to be happy. You can choose happiness now; being grateful for what you have is a great first step toward daily joy.

This week, end each day recording two things for which you're thankful. Mentally scour through your day's events and find two things, people or occurrences that brought you a reason to feel grateful.

It's easier than you think to find acceptance, to trade chaos or confusion for clarity, to realize that you do have enough. Choose to be with each moment and find a way in which you're gifted.

For at least one day this week, turn a not.so.great event in your day into a blessing. Choose to find the silver lining hidden within a tough day or a challenging event from your week.

Week starting:

Day 1

Day 2

Day 3

Day 4

Day 5

Day 6

Day 7

Reflections on my week of gratitude

"I truly believe that everything that we do and everyone that we meet is put in our path for a purpose. There are no accidents; we're all teachers - if we're willing to pay attention to the lessons we learn, trust our positive instincts and not be afraid to take risks or wait for some miracle to come knocking at our door."

~Maria Gibbs

From the moment you were born, you've had teachers in your life. The caregivers who gently held your newly born body were teaching tenderness and love. You always have teachers and influencers around you, coming and going throughout your life. They serve great purpose, and provide you wonderful gifts. You also serve as a teacher in others' lives.

You likely learned mathematics, reading and writing, science and humanities from a traditional teacher in a classroom. But who taught you about love? Kindness? Perseverance? Who taught you to see the beauty in nature and within humankind? Was there a special person who taught you to believe in yourself and your purpose in this world?

Some of life's teachers surprise us. They come in unexpected ways - even in people who annoy or upset us. Their visit to your life might feel frustrating, but it's very intentional and purposeful. It's likely you've had teachers who, through tough life experiences, taught you forgiveness, acceptance, or patience. Although these teachers might have felt unwelcome to your life, they are priceless in teaching the most important, yet difficult, lessons.

This week recall seven important teachers from your life - from the classroom in school to the classroom of life. Who are those people who taught you important lessons, who have left their soulful fingerprint on your heart, who have perhaps challenged you to dig deep within yourself to learn the most difficult lessons? Write one name down each day, and express why you're grateful for the lesson they helped you learn.

This week, be sure to include one of the surprising teachers in your life who perhaps provided you lessons in ways you'd not have expected or wanted. Express gratitude for someone who, although frustrated you, taught you something valuable about life.

Week starting:

Day 1

Day 2

Day 3

Day 4

Day 5

Day 6

Day 7

Reflections on my week of gratitude

"Showing gratitude is one of the simplest yet most powerful things humans can do for each other."

~ **Randy Pausch**

Everyday your life is touched by many people. You may not know the name of your kids' bus driver, the postal service worker, or the young man who serves your favorite morning coffee; but their actions add to your life - they make it easier, safer, more pleasant.

It might be the person at work who always has an upbeat 'Good morning' greeting. Perhaps it's your favorite person at the grocery check out who's always so courteous. There might be a neighbor who sneaks in to mow your lawn before you return from a long day at work. The amount of simple kindness that surrounds you is a tremendous gift that's often overlooked in the rush of life's pace.

The kindness and appreciation you feel or express toward others - even those you don't know well - creates even more kindness and appreciation in the world. Creating a more peaceful and kind world begins with individuals, and even small gestures have great impact. Gratitude makes a difference in the world.

Each day this week record one person who blesses you in some way. Think outside your home, work environment, and close circle of family and friends to those whom you interact on a limited basis. Notice how your life is often blessed, even in small ways, by people you hardly know. Share why you're grateful for such kindness, friendliness, professionalism, or courtesy.

♥ **Gratitude Challenge:** Everyday People

This week go beyond writing your gratitude for every day people in your life. Express thankfulness to at least one of the people on your list. Take a moment to look this person in the eye and say a sincere "Thank you for..."

Week starting:

Day 1

Day 2

Day 3

Day 4

110

Day 5

Day 6

Day 7

Reflections on my week of gratitude

"Appreciation is the highest form of prayer, for it acknowledges the presence of good wherever you shine the light of your thankful thoughts."

~ **Alan Cohen**

Last week you thought about everyday people who bless your life. By thinking outside of your home and immediate circle of family and friends perhaps you remembered many others who touch your life in small ways and help you enjoy each day more.

Every expressed kindness will multiply out into the world. Like the power of a butterfly's wings, your words of thanks, when expressed to others, send a ripple effect of goodness that affect our collective family.

Use this empowerment to spread kindness. It's amazing what a simple conversation or smile can do to lift someone's spirits. This week go beyond thinking and feeling gratitude - express appreciation to those everyday people in your life.

Each day this week, find someone in your day to day interactions to genuinely thank. These people might be from your list created last week or they might be someone not thought of previously. Try expressing your gratitude with more than a simple 'Thank You.'

- For the person who made your dinner, be more explicit - '*I really appreciate when you make such a delicious meal that I can share with you.*'
- Instead of waving to your kids' bus driver, take a moment to lean in to the bus and say, '*Thank you for taking care of my*

kids and getting them safely to and from school - it means a lot to me.'

- Rather than hardly noticing when your co-worker helps you complete your task, tell her, '*Your hard work makes my work easier. I appreciate all the ways you help me each day.'*

As you share deeper, more expressive appreciation to others, you shine the light of gratitude onto someone who'll be lifted by your words. That light continues to travel the world, spreading from one grateful heart to the next.

This week, as you go beyond the typical 'Thank you' to those everyday people in your life, step out of your comfort zone. At least once this week, find someone whom it might be difficult for you to thank.

Week starting:

Day 1

Day 2

Day 3

Day 4

Day 5

Day 6

Day 7

Reflections on my week of gratitude

"Gratitude helps you to grow and expand; gratitude brings joy and laughter into your life and into the lives of all those around you."

~ **Eileen Caddy**

Sometimes you might not feel like growing or expanding. It might feel too difficult or a bit intimidating, but it's the purpose of life - to realize your best self. Gratitude helps you do this as it brings more peace and optimism into life.

Be determined to express gratitude every day. Eventually this way of living - with more appreciation - will become a natural reaction to nearly everything. What a gift you'll give yourself when that's your daily view of life!

This week find and express gratitude for two things from each day. As your day ends, look back at each moment. You'll likely be surprised at how many reasons you find to be happy and smile.

As more and more people live in gratitude, the world becomes a better place. Be a positive influence for this change and encourage others to be thankful every day, too!

As you recount your day and record at least two reasons for which to find gratitude, go a step further. Encourage one person this week to share gratitude. You can do this with a simple conversation, sharing what you're doing in this journal, or you can subtly ask, *"What are two things from your day that made you feel happy?"*

Week starting:

Day 1

Day 2

Day 3

Day 4

Day 5

Day 6

Day 7

Reflections on my week of gratitude

"You may say that I'm a dreamer, but I'm not the only one. I hope someday you'll join us. And the world will live as one."

~ **John Lennon**

Where would we be without dreamers? The people who dream about new ways of doing things change the ways we live and help each other. Dreaming is the first step to creating something fresh - whether it's something for the whole world or for one person.

Who is someone you know who's dreaming? Perhaps they're dreaming of something for the world - a new way of providing education, clean water, or safe shelter. Maybe they're dreaming of something for their personal life - a new business venture or education, a loving relationship, or a healthy body.

Dreaming is the first stage of creation - without that step, there would never be anything new. Dreams thrive when there are people cheering for their realization.

When you see someone working toward a dream, it might feel like there's nothing you can do. After all, it's their life, choices, and actions that will create their experiences. But you can help. You can offer support, even from afar.

There are a few ways you can do this. This week think of one person who has a big dream - someone you can cheer on all week. Or think of seven people who are working toward dreams - support one each day of the upcoming week.

Write the person's name on a day of the week, and for each day choose one of the following ideas to support their dream or goal:

119

You can say a little prayer, envision their success, write a quick note of encouragement, or offer to help in some small away. Be grateful for all the world's dreams - those who are out in the world birthing new ideas and dreams.

Think of your own dream... what would you like to create? Spend ten minutes dreaming and writing down ideas for how you can bring your dream to life!

Week starting:

Day 1

Day 2

Day 3

Day 4

Day 5

Day 6

Day 7

Reflections on my week of gratitude

"Thousands of candles can be lighted from a single candle, and the life of the candle will not be shortened. Happiness never decreases by being shared."

~ **Buddha**

How can you share something intangible, like happiness? There are many ways to do so. This week you're going to think of seven!

I bet there are at least seven people in your life who could use a little lift, a small gesture of kindness, a tiny act of thoughtfulness. Aim to spread happiness by spending no money or very little.

Perhaps your co-worker loves a particular candy. Buy some, walk up to him and say, "I thought you might enjoy a little treat. Have a nice day!"

Maybe your neighbor loves fresh flowers. Stop by with a few daisies in your hand and a smile on your face.

Does a friend need some encouragement in her life? Send a quick note telling her how great and beautiful and smart and lovely she is. Tell her you believe in her and love her.

Does your child love collecting rocks from the beach? Go for a walk and find the best stone to bring back for him.

Happiness is contagious. It starts within each of us, is simple to share, and multiplies not only in the one who receives it, but also in the one who gives. As the Buddha stated, sharing your happiness with others will never diminish your own joy.

For each day this week, record the name of someone who you gave a little extra happiness to and how you did it. Remember, it can be as simple as a big smile or a welcomed hug!

Is there someone in your life with whom you don't always get along? Maybe there's an individual who you just had a disagreement with? Find a small way to extend happiness to this person. It might be just what it takes to start softening the tension between you.

Week starting:

Day 1

Day 2

Day 3

Day 4

Day 5

Day 6

Day 7

Reflections on my week of gratitude

"Hope is the thing with feathers that perches in the soul - and sings the tunes without the words - and never stops at all."

~ **Emily Dickinson**

I know someone who could use a little hope. Someone...
who has never really felt passionate love in her life.
who is slowly losing his eyesight.
who lacks confidence in herself.
who has always wanted to have a child but can't conceive.
who has been struggling with chronic pain from a car accident
for over fourteen years.
who feels lost in life - feeling like he has no purpose.
who is drinking so much that his life is fading away to a blur.
who is coping with an eating disorder.

Who do you know? Who needs some hope?

Most of us have witnessed someone walking through a major
life struggle. Sometimes those life events - struggles that are very
frightening or tragic - can seem to define someone or leave an
indelible mark on their ability to be joyful.

This week think about seven people who are struggling in some
way. What do you wish for each person? What hope do you have
for their lives and futures? For each day, record one person's
name and your hope-filled wish for him or her. Then close your
eyes and say a little prayer or feel some hope for each. You might
even try to envision this person experiencing your wish coming
true.

127

Perhaps this person doesn't even know that you want something good for him or her. That's okay! They don't need to know - in fact, it's fun just holding that hope in your heart. Imagine if our world was filled with people wishing good things for others!

Think of someone whom you do not know - perhaps someone you've read about or learned about on the news. What hope can you give this person? What kindness or joy do you wish for this person?

Week starting:

Day 1

Day 2

Day 3

Day 4

Day 5

Day 6

Day 7

Reflections on my week of gratitude

"Everything we do should be a result of our gratitude for what God has done for us."

~ **Lauryn Hill**

People sometimes think bad things happen 'to us' - like punishment or revenge, and good things happen 'for us' - like rewards or celebrations. Yet nothing happens 'to' us; everything happens 'for' us - for us to become the best people we're possible of being. A 'for us' attitude or approach to life, allows us to experience life with acceptance and a mind open to the question 'how does this event help me learn, grow, and realize my best self?'

This attitude might be a struggle on certain days. Perhaps someone says something hurtful to you. Maybe something happens that results in you feeling anger, grief, loneliness, or hopelessness. You might even find yourself wondering why you're having a particular ongoing struggle in life.

In those moments when it feels like difficult emotions are defeating you, shift your perspective. Rather than remain stuck in thoughts and a view point that brings you down, choose to view your experience from a fresh perspective.

For instance, if you really love someone or a career, but this person or opportunity leaves you, you'll likely have some heavy emotions. However, if you choose to view it differently - with a fresh perspective and as an opportunity to learn - you'll have renewed hope. Perhaps in the loss of this person or opportunity, you'll find more joy, love or a better opportunity. You can choose to trust that life is directing you toward new experiences that will bring you even more peace and joy. You have the power to choose your perspective.

Every day this week find three reasons to be grateful. As you head to bed, review your day and regardless of how it felt - easy or difficult - express thankfulness and trust that you're guided to realize your best self. See how life is happening 'for us' rather than 'to us.'

At least one time this week find a struggle, even if you need to recall one from weeks, months or years previously, and find a reason to be grateful. This event might have felt like it happened 'to' you, but you can shift your perspective to see how it happened 'for' you to grow and learn.

Week starting:

Day 1

Day 2

Day 3

Day 4

Day 5

Day 6

Day 7

Reflections on my week of gratitude

Part of Appreciating Others with gratitude means working through forgiveness and being more compassionate.

I've created a few free gifts for you - to help you learn my favorite tips for forgiving others, how to practice compassion which will bless you and others more than you can imagine, and a fun way to practice gratitude while you're out and about in the world.

Go to http://shannonelhart.com/gratitude-others/ to enjoy them!

Experiencing the World

"I am convinced that material things can contribute a lot to making one's life pleasant, but, basically, if you do not have very good friends and relatives who matter to you, life will be really empty and sad and material things cease to be important."

~ **David Rockefeller**

You probably realize that the material things in life are nothing in comparison to the people and joy you experience. Yet there are times when you might wish for more, perhaps yearning for others' possessions.

There are simple things in life people might take for granted. Perhaps you have a very soft bed to rest on each night. Maybe it's a collection of great books that take you away from the day. to.day hustle. It might even be something that brings you a lot of fun such as a boat or cottage on a river.

Rather than think about things you wish for, focus on gratitude for all you already have. Most material things aren't necessary for your survival or even your joy. Your life is blessed in many ways with the items that surround you. It might be something as simple as the coffee maker that brews your favorite morning cup each day or the comfortable chair you rest on at night while you unwind.

This week find gratitude for the material things in your life and in your surroundings without desiring more. Each day choose an item you're grateful for and record why you're happy it's part of your life. Remember you're blessed to have these items, and recognize that a common thing in your life might be considered a luxury to others.

On at least one day this week express gratitude for a simple item that brings you comfort or joy. Look differently at something as common as a plush blanket or photo, seeing it as a true gift that uplifts you in subtle ways.

Week starting:

_____

Day 1

_____

Day 2

_____

Day 3

_____

Day 4

Day 5

Day 6

Day 7

Reflections on my week of gratitude

"Each day provides its own gifts."

~ **Marcus Aurelius**

It's true; each day is a gift. With every day that you're moving and breathing, loving and creating, you can be filled with gratitude for simply being alive. It's life itself, not things, that bring true joy. Still, there are likely those little things around you that make you smile as you recall a special event or a tender memory.

You've probably received meaningful gifts from others - perhaps even from yourself. These treasures, small expressions of love, lift your heart. Although they don't define your joy, you can be grateful to hold them in your hand!

This week, find seven items that bring you a smile. Perhaps it's a meaningful piece of jewelry or a photograph of a loved one. You might feel a flutter of happiness every time you use a teacup from your grandmother or see the pottery given to you from a child. Perhaps there's a letter tucked away in your nightstand, that when reread brings a few tears of joy. On your journal pages, record why you're grateful to have this item in your life.

While you search your home for small items you appreciate, find something special and give it to someone else to enjoy. Sometimes it's difficult to give away something treasured, but you'll feel great as you pass it to someone new who'll now begin treasuring it from you!

Week starting:

Day 1

Day 2

Day 3

Day 4

Day 5

Day 6

Day 7

Reflections on my week of gratitude

"Habit converts luxurious enjoyments into dull and daily necessities."

~ **Aldous Huxley**

Everyone gets into ruts sometimes. You might rush from one event to another and then another, and before you know it, the sun has set on another day. A part of your routine, which might be considered a luxury to many, can be overlooked and unappreciated. Begin to feel gratitude for all the simple pleasures in your life.

Living in a country such as the United States, most people are blessed more than they realize. There are comforts and perks galore. Here are some statistics to that might surprise you:

In 2013-14:

- 780 million people lacked access to clean water (that's more than 2.5 times the United States population)
- Almost half the world lived on less than $2.50 each day
- Nearly one billion people, in 2000, were unable to read a book or sign their own name
- One in three children throughout the world lacked adequate shelter
- A quarter of humanity lived without electricity

* globalissues.org
* water.org

This week, look around you, pay attention to how easily your tasks are accomplished, how swiftly your basic needs are met. Then, at the end of each day, record one luxury, perhaps not normally viewed as a luxury, you have in your life and why you're grateful for it.

Perhaps you realize how wonderful it is to get from one place to another so easily, using your own car, public transport, or a bicycle. The fact that you can walk into your kitchen and find healthy food at any time is a pure blessing! The comforts of your home, clean and safe water to drink and to bathe, a comfortable bed, carpeted floors... are all much more than many people have, and undeniably, much more than anyone needs to live a full and happy life.

This week express gratitude for seven things that bless your life beyond necessity. Be creative - look for those things that seem to pass you by unnoticed but that you surely enjoy!

Make a donation this week to an agency that works to provide basic needs - food, water, shelter, education - to those less fortunate than yourself.

Week starting:

Day 1

Day 2

Day 3

Day 4

Day 5

Day 6

Day 7

Reflections on my week of gratitude

"Gratitude to gratitude always gives birth."

~ Sophocles

What do you want to bring into your life? What do you wish to experience? Is it more love or opportunity? A healed relationship? Hope for your future or peace with your past? Perhaps it is something you can hold in your hands. Maybe it is something you'd like to give to another person.

When you live in a place of wanting, without remembering to be grateful for all you have, you're left with only desire. When you express appreciation, you open the door to experiencing more.

This week reflect on your gratitude for being grateful. That might sound odd, but in The Healing Gift of Gratitude, you've chosen to shift your perspective. Be grateful for this shift in your life. You'll give birth to even more - more gratitude, joy, peace - and pure acceptance for all of life.

As each day comes to an end, look back at your journey so far this year and recognize ways in which you've grown. You have now been consciously expressing gratitude for ten months. That's approximately 300 days that you've ended with a smile and lightness in your heart!

What differences are you feeling? Do you feel more accepting of life? Do you feel more calm and peace? Are you experiencing more trust and joy each day? Are others noticing a change in you? Are you living with less anxiety? Are you more satisfied with what you have rather than wanting more?

This week express at least three things that you're grateful for each day. Focus on ways in which you're growing in gratitude this year.

♥ **Gratitude Challenge:** Personal Daily Reflection

Think back to your perspective on gratitude when you began this year of gratitude journey. At least one time this week, record a few ways in which your overall view has shifted to more thankfulness and appreciation.

Week starting:

Day 1

Day 2

Day 3

Day 4

Day 5

Day 6

Day 7

Reflections on my week of gratitude

"Sunshine is delicious, rain is refreshing, wind braces us up, snow is exhilarating; there is really no such thing as bad weather, only different kinds of weather."

~ **John Ruskin**

This week, notice more of the beauty surrounding you in the natural world of weather. We often overlook the gifts of sunshine on our faces, a powerful rain storm, or the cooling shade of a cloud.

It can be frustrating when storm clouds block the sunshine or when cold temperatures halt a flower's bloom. If a certain day or a season's weather isn't what we expect, we often feel disappointed.

The gift you'll give yourself this week, is a shift in perspective from disappointment to appreciation of the earth's weather - all of it: sunshine and rain, the sweltering heat of summer and the brisk winds of winter.

Many people, mostly out of habit, say it's a *'bad day'* when it's raining. But where would we be without rain? All life needs the earth to be drenched with life-sustaining water. When you change your perspective, even if it falls on your wedding day, you empower yourself with acceptance and a positive outlook.

This week, begin viewing all of the earth's weather as a gift - each day, find gratitude in the world and its weather around you, knowing how blessed you are to live in such diverse experiences.

At least one time this week, find appreciation for an aspect of weather that you've previously thought of as annoying or inconvenient. Recognize it as part of the necessary, natural, beautiful ways in which Earth supports life.

Week starting:

Day 1

Day 2

Day 3

Day 4

Day 5

Day 6

Day 7

Reflections on my week of gratitude

"Until one has loved an animal a part of one's soul remains unawakened."

~ **Anatole France**

Animals provide our world with so many gifts. Without the amazing diversity of the animal kingdom, we'd have fewer sources of beauty, compassion, and awe. It's easy to enjoy animals that are in your life or environment, but there are many more to appreciate beyond the border of your own backyard or community.

Pets that are loved as part of your family are special, and they bring happiness and fun into many homes. The majestic lion, graceful deer, or mighty elephant are also easily admired. However, there are many other animals that bless our environments in countless ways.

Without bees, the pollination of plants would suffer. Spiders create their beautiful artwork but also help bring relief from insects. Even pesky moles do their work by eating bugs that can destroy the roots of flowers. Each animal's life holds purpose, each animal provides the world with gifts.

This week, express gratitude for the animal kingdom. Although you might include animals that are in your day to day life, look beyond them to consider animals from around the world. Recognize that each animal is a part of our circle of life.

For one day this week, even if you're someone who greatly enjoys eating animal products, such as meat, eggs, milk, and cheese, go without. For that day, eat only foods that do not require anything of the animal kingdom. You might miss or crave those foods, but each time you do, express gratitude for all the ways in which the animal kingdom blesses our world.

Week starting:

Day 1

Day 2

Day 3

Day 4

Day 5

Day 6

Day 7

Reflections on my week of gratitude

"I thank you God for this most amazing day, for the leaping greenly spirit of trees, and for the blue dream of sky and for everything which is natural, which is infinite, which is yes."

~ e.e. cummings

This week, take note of the natural beauty that surrounds you. It can be easy to overlook the sunshine, walk past blooming flowers without noting their fragrance, or hardly notice the breeze against your body.

Regardless of our environment, we can be reminded every day of the beauty in our world. Wherever you are, simply look up, and see our marvelous, unending sky, changing in each moment with wind-tossed clouds or sparkling sunshine.

You might notice grand aspects of nature - the awe of standing at the base of a mountain or a waterfall cascading along its side. Perhaps you'll note subtler parts of nature - sitting by a water's edge, listening to the soft lap of waves or trickle of a stream. Maybe you'll enjoy a cup of tea as thunder rolls in, and you feel the first refreshing sprinkle of a storm. You could even scan your memory or a book of nature photography to recall the world's magnificence.

This week, view all of nature - the movement of our elements, the beauty of the forests, meadows, mountains and waters - as a gift... a gift for you and all of life to enjoy and cherish.

Take note of one aspect of nature you've underappreciated. Recognize a tree's strength, the resilience of a forest, or the perseverance of a flower bursting through a busy sidewalk.

Week starting:

Day 1

Day 2

Day 3

Day 4

Day 5

Day 6

Day 7

Reflections on my week of gratitude

160

"All those hours exploring the great outdoors made me more resilient and confident."

~ **David Suzuki**

In this busy world where so much happens indoors, this week celebrate what you love about being outdoors. Without even realizing it, you can become stuck in a routine that doesn't allow you to be outside enjoying fresh air and nature.

Being outside makes us better connected to ourselves and the world, and helps us be healthier, more appreciative of Earth, and naturally energized. There are many wonderful things you can enjoy outside - taking advantage of your natural surroundings is easier than you might think.

Whether you live in a bustling city or a small town, step out your front door and go for a walk. Leave your technology behind and enjoy the chirping birds and rustling leaves. Get some exercise by jogging or kayaking. Explore the space around your home. Consider walking barefoot through your grass. Start a simple garden, even one with only a few potted plants can be a lot of fun. Sit beneath a tree and read. Ask a friend to meet you for a walk through a park or forest. Take a new perspective by lying on the ground to relax and watch the passing clouds. Find some flowers to look at, touch, and smell. Go outdoors and breathe!

Take time this week to celebrate things you enjoy about being outside. Each day remind yourself to go outside for at least ten minutes. Do whatever you're drawn to do, and then be present. Take in the environment and experience with all your senses. Record what you did and why you're grateful to be able to do it.

Try something new this week - take a new path to walk, find a different way of exercising outside, ask a new friend to walk with you around the neighborhood, or plant a tree.

Week starting:

Day 1

Day 2

Day 3

Day 4

Day 5

Day 6

Day 7

Reflections on my week of gratitude

"Silent gratitude isn't very much to anyone."

~ **Gertrude Stein**

Expressing gratitude to others is powerful, especially for those who hear your words. It's also transforming to hear your thankful voice each day expressing gratitude for your life.

Negative thoughts affect your happiness - and are more defeating when spoken aloud. The same is true of positive thinking. Whether they're affirmations or expressions of gratitude, when spoken aloud you're better able to soak in the truth of those thoughts.

Don't be afraid of your voice when you sit in a room alone. It's a vital part of you and an important aspect of your expression and uniqueness. Just like your fingerprints, your voice is part of your identity, and it can be used to bring a lot of good into the world around you.

This week, write your thoughts of gratitude. Then take one more step - quietly speak them aloud. Softly whisper them or stand tall and state them with a strong, confident voice. Whether whispered to yourself or yelled from a mountain top, speaking your thoughts of gratitude aloud is like saying a little prayer.

At least once this week, ask someone to tell you about something they're gratitude for from the day. If you have children, this is a wonderful practice to share and encourage in their daily life. Kids might not want to write their gratitude in a journal, but they typically enjoy speaking about it!

Week starting:

Day 1

Day 2

Day 3

Day 4

Day 5

Day 6

Day 7

Reflections on my week of gratitude

"I can hardly sleep. I feel my target now is really to save Mother Earth for humanity. And it's doable."

~ **Imelda Marcos**

Earth is a gift, and we're blessed to spend our lives enjoying her beauty. As a global community it's critical that we save Earth from decisions that hurt our natural home - a home shared by all of life, not just humans. Saving her *is* doable!

Remain hopeful that with each passing year, progress is made to restore our natural environment. Wonderful initiatives are helping people learn of ways to help. Simple choices, such as recycling, reusing, or minimizing our use of resources are becoming a common practice. Organizations work to protect environments and animals, and individuals devote their lives to creating a healthier world for all of life.

This week, focus on the positive actions taken to protect, heal, and nourish Mother Earth. Although there are still choices that diminish her health and vitality, keep your attention on the good being done. Each day, record a positive action or step that's helping - be creative and look for new approaches. Then express why you're grateful for these optimistic actions.

As you do a quick search for alternative tips on saving Earth, commit to adding one of these tips to your life. For example - are you composting yet? Are you minimizing the electricity you use? Have you given away the things you don't really need and vowed to limit purchases? What about stopping that lawn service that sends chemicals into our waterways - have you cancelled it yet?

Week starting:

Day 1

Day 2

Day 3

Day 4

Day 5

Day 6

Day 7

Reflections on my week of gratitude

"When you forgive, you do not change the past, but you change the future."

~ **Unknown**

Forgiveness is one of the most powerful actions you can take throughout life. Everyone suffers - some pain has been at the hands of another person; some is from your own hands through decisions and actions you've chosen. Pain also comes simply from the circumstances that enter your life. This is part of the duality of life that teaches and guides you. Without pain, you'd appreciate joy less.

When you forgive yourself or another person, you become free. You release yourself from regret, shame, guilt, anger, or resentment. Forgiveness frees you from wishing the past was different. It frees you from seeking revenge, proving you're right, or receiving an apology.

Forgiving someone has nothing to do with the other person. It's about *you* - freeing yourself to move forward without the shackles of past pain and anger.

Forgiveness is also about the world. Each time someone forgives, there is more light in the world. There is less pain, anger, and resentment. When we experience a world with more joy, there will be an overall change that will benefit all life.

This week, find events or people from your past that you will release - things for which you will forgive yourself or someone else. If you need help, find it through a trusted friend, counselor, or another source that teaches forgiveness. This will be a decision, not a feeling. Choose to forgive, and trust that forgiveness will come - even if it takes more time. On your journal pages, record your forgiveness actions each day and why you're grateful to have this choice.

If it's safe and comfortable to do so, express your forgiveness to someone in your life. Be sure this person is ready to receive your forgiveness. When two people express and receive forgiveness, the light you give the world is more than doubled.

Week starting:

Day 1

Day 2

Day 3

Day 4

Day 5

Day 6

Day 7

Reflections on my week of gratitude

"For it is in giving that we receive."

~ **St. Francis of Assisi**

In many cultures around the world, people have an abundance of things. Many are necessary or helpful; some are meaningful or sentimental - but most are unnecessary.

This week, look around your environment. Find seven things that have blessed your life in some way but are no longer needed. You might find an article of clothing or jewelry. Look in your kitchen for few items you no longer use. There's a chance you might even notice some great art or even a piece of furniture or equipment that no longer fits your decor.

As long as these items are in good shape, someone else could use and enjoy them. Take time to look around each day to find something you no longer use, and decide where to donate it. Record these items and include why you're grateful to have had it or glad to gift it to someone else to use.

You'll receive more than expected: the joy of helping others, the ease of more simplicity in your home, and the knowledge that you're benefitting the world by reusing items rather than tossing them into landfills.

Minimizing personal possessions is a popular topic for good reason - it helps in financial and Earth-friendly ways, and it saves you time. The less you accumulate, the less money you spend and the less you have to maintain. This week, along with donating unused items, consider how you can begin living differently by buying and living with less.

Week starting:

Day 1

Day 2

Day 3

Day 4

Day 5

Day 6

Day 7

Reflections on my week of gratitude

"Invite me to an anti-war rally, and I will not go. Invite me to a peace rally, and I'll be there."

~ **Mother Teresa**

"All you need is love... Love is all you need."

~ **The Beatles**

You're almost done with your year of gratitude and healing! To celebrate, we're spending the next two weeks doing something special.

The loosely quoted thought from Mother Teresa is a favorite of mine. It reminds me where to keep my focus, which is a choice I make every day.

Many people might think that anti-war and peace rallies are the same, but they are very different. Take a moment to imagine an anti.war rally. What do you see?

You likely see people expressing anger, sadness, frustration, and panic. You probably feel hopelessness, pressure, and fear.

Now, imagine a peace rally.

Quite different, aren't they? The peace rally was likely filled with hope, love, kindness, acceptance, calm, trust, and gentleness. This brings me to the second quote from the Beatles, "All you need is Love."

If you're at an anti.war rally, you're giving more energy to war rather than bringing peace. If you want to provide peace to the world, give more energy to peace... not to anti.war.

Choose which rally to live in. You can move through each day with the emotions and perspective of an anti.war rally. You might even convince yourself that you're doing good when you complain about politics or the weather. You might justify the gossip at work, the continued anger between you and someone else, the persistent fear that fuels your anxiety about the future.

Or move through your day as if it were a peace rally framed with love. hope, joy, and peace. Live with purpose and intention. Trust that your life is unfolding perfectly even when things are uncomfortable or painful. Release shame. Forgive others. Treat all of life with respect and kindness. Leave others with a smile on their face from interacting with you. The more people who choose to live with love and peace, the greater opportunity we have to create a peaceful world.

This week focus on giving love to the world. Each day, think about something or someone who needs love - an environment, a country, a group of people, animals, or an individual. Allow your mind and intuition to guide you.

Then sit for 2-3 minutes focusing on giving love to the object of your thoughts. Feel your heart opening, allow the love to flow from you to the world. This might seem strange, but try it. Trust that it works. You are energy, so send your best energy into the world.

All WE need is Love... more Love in the world. Be that Love.

In your journal, record who you gave love to and how it felt to share it.

Don't judge your experiences from this practice, don't wonder if you're doing it 'right'... just do it! Open your heart, step into the peace rally of hope, joy, peace and love... and give it to the world. Love will never run out; it'll only grow more abundant as it's shared.

For some extra guidance, listen to my loving-kindness meditation. It will guide you through giving more love, peace, and kindness to yourself, others, and the entire world. You can find it at <u>www.shannonelhart.com/lovekind</u>

Week starting:

Day 1

Day 2

Day 3

Day 4

Day 5

Day 6

Day 7

Reflections on my week of gratitude

181

"We can never obtain peace in the outer world until we make peace within ourselves."

~ **Dalai Lama**

I hope you enjoyed sharing love with others last week. You made a difference - we all do when we choose to express love in our life.

Our bodies and thoughts are energy, so it's important to be aware of what we're giving the world. Think about a time when you felt a 'bad vibe' from someone and wanted to turn in the opposite direction. Think of a person with whom you felt an immediate connection and developed a great new friendship or love relationship. *That* is energy.

We all carry energy, and we give it to the people and the world around us. Currently there are many people sharing negative energy of anger, sadness, and fear.

This week, focus on the tremendous need for peace in our world. Every day, spend 2-3 minutes finding peace within yourself and then giving it to others.

Focus on yourself for a day or two. What issue or relationship in your life is not at peace? Hold that experience or person in your mind, search for peace within you, then give that peace to both yourself and the other. It might not resolve the issue, but it's at least the beginning of peace.

Next, move on to others. You probably know of a person or group who's suffering. Send those people peace by capturing it within you and intending their suffering to cease. If you think of people who cause suffering, send them peace, too. If someone's heart is truly at peace, they won't want to cause suffering for others.

Think of people in your life who need peace with an illness, strained relationships, job loss, financial struggles, or the death of a loved one. Who do you know who needs more peace right now?

Take a bigger step and imagine the entire world in your hands. Give the peace within you a color, have that color surround and cover the entire planet. Imagine the peace from your heart blessing the entire world.

From now on, when you learn of suffering in the world, take a moment to stop, close your eyes, tap into your peace, and send it to those who need it. That'll do more good than feeling anger or fear over the suffering you hear of in the world.

In your journal, record who you gave peace to, then share how this felt each day.

You might feel like you're too small to make a big difference in the world. That's not true. You are powerful, and so is your energy. To bring peace to those around you and to the entire world, you need to be peace within. Each day spend time bringing more peace into your body, mind, and spirit. You can do so by simply relaxing your body, closing your eyes, focusing on your breathing, and on every inhale repeat, "I am peace."

Week starting:

Day 1

Day 2

Day 3

Day 4

Day 5

Day 6

Day 7

Reflections on my week of gratitude

"Let gratitude be the pillow upon which you kneel to say your nightly prayer."

~ Maya Angelou

Congratulations on reaching your final week of The Healing Gift of Gratitude! I hope you've enjoyed this year, and that it's blessed you abundantly.

Gratitude has become a very important part of my life - it has shaped how I live and it gave purpose to this book. So much of my personal healing and happiness have come from learning to find and express gratitude even during my darkest times. My life is much better because I've learned to find and focus upon the good in myself, others, and the world around me.

In practicing gratitude, I've learned to trust God, the universe and the rhythm of life. I've also learned to trust my relationships with others, to take actions less personally and grow in compassion and acceptance. I've learned what's truly important in life. I've loosened my grip on the past, resentments, the need for control, fear, anger, and my personal view point. I've healed a lot of pain from earlier in my life which has allowed me to create a happier today. Gratitude has opened me to be a better person in every way.

Thank you for taking this year to grow in gratitude and begin a process of healing emotional pain. It's an honor to be your gentle guide, and I hope you've found many gifts from living a more thankful life.

I believe in peace for our world, and I'm certain that true peace begins within each individual heart. Continue finding and expressing your thankfulness each day, and your heart will grow to be more peaceful; then you'll bless the world with the peace from within your heart.

End each day of this final week with your knees resting gently on a pillow of gratitude. Express your gratitude as a prayer to the world. Trust that in doing so, you make a difference. Every day gather and record as many reasons as you can to be grateful for another day of life.

My wish for you - may peace, love, hope, joy and gratitude fill your life always,

~ **Shannon Elhart**

Make a promise to yourself that you'll always heal the pain that arises in your life - whether it needs acceptance or forgiveness - be patient but persistent in your healing. As more people live a life free from the pain in the past, we'll see less pain being created among us. Also promise to live the rest of life with a grateful heart. There are always reasons to be thankful. Find at least one each day and feel it fully.

Week starting:

___

Day 1

___

Day 2

___

Day 3

___

Day 4

Day 5

Day 6

Day 7

Reflections on my week of gratitude

Healing the pain in your life and living with gratitude will help you Experience the World from a place of inner peace and hope. Now more than ever we need people living from this new perspective. We need more people like **you**!

I've created a few more free gifts for you. Use the link below to learn how you can heal the pain from your past and continue your journey with gratitude!

For these wonderful free gifts go to <u>www.shannonelhart.com/</u><u>gratitude-world</u>

67290884R00121

Made in the USA
Lexington, KY
07 September 2017